Mums the W

Secrets to Growing Chrysan
For Home or Show

PAT STOCKETT JOHNSTON

 My husband Gordon is the silent type. He's my quiet mums-growing partner. He transfers plants to larger pots, and carries the full responsibility for watering, fertilizing, and spraying for unwanted creatures. So we're a team. There would be no chrysanthemums growing at the Johnston Joint without him. "Thanks, Babe!"

Shortly after Pat was elected President of the National Chrysanthemum Society, Inc., USA in October 2015 she suddenly passed away. Her heirs have graciously transferred the copyright for this book to our organization. We thank them for this wonderful gesture and are thankful that we can continue the publication of Pat's book. Pat loved her mums and our organization. We miss her and her wisdom. To learn more about our organization and growing mums, please go to our website at www.mums.org.

Mums the Word: Secrets to Growing Chrysanthemums for Home or Show
© 2018 National Chrysanthemum Society, Inc., USA

All rights reserved. No part of this publication may be reproduced in any form without written permission from the National Chrysanthemum Society Inc., USA

ISBN 978-1482534399

Photograph of Spider Mum on pg. 6 used with permission from *Kings Mums* catalog.
Photographs of rooted cuttings on pg. 7 used with permission from *Kings Mums* catalog.

Photographs: copyright, 2012 by Pat Stockett Johnston
Cover Design by Alison Anderson, http://www.bluepeacockcreative.com
Photographs on cover by Dale A. Welcome, http://www.flickr.com/photos/welcomephotoimages

Table of Contents

Introduction 1

   Chapter 1: My First Try at Growing Mums 3

   Chapter 2: Tasks for March - April - May 6

   Chapter 3: Tasks for June - July 13

   Chapter 4: Tasks for August 16

   Chapter 5: Tasks for September 21

   Chapter 6: Tasks for October 27

   Chapter 7: Getting Ready to Exhibit: October - November 30

   Chapter 8: Judging Mum Blooms: October - November 34

   Chapter 9: Plant Care for January - February 36

King's Pleasure – Class 1 Irregular Incurve

Introduction

I've never considered myself to be a gardener, as every living plant that took up abode in my house died within the first month. But now my favorite fall hobby is growing chrysanthemums (mums) for home and show exhibitions. You may wonder how that happened. By accident!

My husband and I visited Descanso Gardens in La Cañada Flintridge, CA, on the first weekend of November 2004 and wandered into Van De Kamp Hall to view the Descanso Chrysanthemum Society Show. I was expecting bunches of the popular garden mums with their small flowers. Instead we walked up and down rows of huge blooms, each in their own vase, gracing the Hall with their beauty. We walked each row, oohing and aweing over the magnificent display.

Toward the end of our tour through those fabulous mums, we were attracted to a bright, chartreuse Kermit pompon spray. We had never seen a plant that produced green blooms. I asked Descanso Chrysanthemum Society member Jay Pengra, "How can we learn to grow these beautiful flowers?" He told us to join the Society, attend monthly meetings, and the members would show us. So we paid our dues, and since then have regularly attended monthly meetings. I'm now the president of the Descanso Chrysanthemum Society and an accredited National

Chrysanthemum Society (NCS) judge. We enjoy gifting our friends and neighbors with beautiful mum blooms every fall, and we enter blooms in three local NCS Shows a year.

What I Love About Chrysanthemums[1]

One of the most exciting things about growing chrysanthemums for home and show is the huge variety of blooms (cultivars in botanical terms) available through Kings Mums Catalog or local Societies. The following pictures show a bloom grown from each of the 13 chrysanthemum classes.

Crimson Tide — Class 1 – Irregular Incurve
Peach Wingfield — Class 2 – Reflex
Moira — Class 3 – Regular Incurve
Resomee Purple — Class 4 – Decorative
Seaton's J'dore — Class 5 – Intermediate Incurve
Yoko Ono — Class 6 - Pompon
Peggy Stevens — Class 7 – Singles/Semi-doubles
Daybreak — Class 8 - Anemone
Redwing — Class 9 – Spoons
Seatons Toffee — Class 10 – Quill
Icicles — Class 11 – Spiders
Aoi — Class 12 – Brush & Thistle
Diana Stokes — Class 13 - Exotic

Chapter one of *Mums the Word: Secrets for Growing Chrysanthemums for Home or Show* describes my successes and failures the first year I grew mums. The remaining chapters discuss the monthly tasks of growing mums for home or show. Chapter 2 begins with the March – April - May tasks because spring is the time of year to start the process of growing these fall blooms. Follow this book's directions and you, too, will learn how to grow large, gorgeous chrysanthemum blooms that will brighten your garden, make beautiful floral arrangements, and qualify for entry in exhibition shows.

---

[1] View video: Pat Stockett Johnston YouTube - The 13 Classes of Chrysanthemums Grown for Exhibitions

Chapter 1
My First Try at Growing Mums

As a new member, the Descanso Chrysanthemum Society presented me with six free rooted cuttings to get me started on the road to growing chrysanthemums for home and show. I bought one more at the Society's yearly May plant sale, for a grand total of seven. Because of the 100% failure rate of my previous house and garden plants, I held little hope of those seven baby plants surviving, under my care, for more than a month.

Early in the growing season we newbies learned about the 13 classes of chrysanthemums. We were taught the difference between the two main types of blooms we could grow with our free cuttings: either a *disbud* or a *spray*. We were told some cultivars could be grown as both a disbud and a spray.

The Difference Between a "Disbud" and a "Spray"

Disbud: *River City* -- Class 1

The greatest portion of show mums are grown as disbuds, meaning only one bud is allowed to bloom on a stem. This style requires all but one flower bud be disbudded (removed) from the stem of the maturing plant. That's why a single bloom on one stem is called a "disbud." Six of my first-year mum plants were the disbud variety.

Spray: *Saga Nishiki* -- Class 12

A "spray" is grown on one mum stem and is required to have five or more blooms. Each bloom must grow on its own stem (pedicel in botanical terms). The center bloom should be as tall as or taller than the other blooms in the spray. Some mum cultivars can be grown as both a disbud and a spray, especially class 6 and 12.

3

First Year Blue Ribbon Winners

Lavender Pixie Spray   **Purple Light Disbud**   **Seatons Toffee Disbud**   **Bill Holden Disbud**
Won Best Novice Trophy   **Class 7 Anemone**   **Class 10 Quill**   **Class 2 Reflex**

Growing Chrysanthemums Costs

Growing chrysanthemums for home or show does require the purchase of potting soil, rooting powder or concentrate, fertilizer, systemic and spray insecticides, fungicides, 2", 4", 6" and 10" pots, and stakes. We spent about $50.00 that first year on supplies. The beauty of the blooms was worth every penny.

Pat's 2005 Entries in the Novice Section

The Descanso Chrysanthemum Society Exhibition Show arrived the first week of November. Amazingly, all seven of my mum plants had survived. The judges are always kind to novices, and my entries received four blue ribbons, two red ribbons, and one a card that said "Judged." I was thrilled. If I can successfully grow mums for my garden, flower arrangements, and exhibition shows, so can you!

My First Year Growing Mums Mistakes

I correctly put the stem stakes holding the center blooms in straight. But the remaining two stem stakes are inserted at an angle. Stakes should not be slanted outward in the pot. Each stake should be vertical (straight up).

Notice how closely the three stakes are placed in this pot.
The stakes should be place in a triangle shape equal distances apart.

    The missing leaves on the stem of this quill mum were probably knocked off when tying the stem to the stake. I didn't know the leaves were important.
    The stem is not straight because it wasn't tied to the stake soon enough in the growing process.

Exhibition blooms need to stand 22 inches high on the display tables.

Notice how out-of-proportion this Bola de Oro Class 1 incurve bloom is to the stem height. That's because the stem was cut too short.

Chapter 2: March - April - May

Growing Mums from Purchased Rooted Cuttings

Mums are fall flowers that bloom in September, October, and November. This book does not describe how to grow the common garden variety of mums. The National Chrysanthemum Society website answers questions about growing garden mums.[2]

Mums the Word explains how the 13 classes of chrysanthemums can be grown for the home garden, flower arrangements, and exhibition shows. Seeds cannot be purchased for these 13 classes of mums. They are grown from cuttings. An easy way to obtain rooted mum cuttings is to buy them from a catalog such as *Kings Mums* (www.kingsmums.com). The Kings Mums company website has pictures of over 200 different mum blooms (cultivars) for which rooted cuttings can be purchased online.

Steps for Growing Purchased Rooted Cuttings

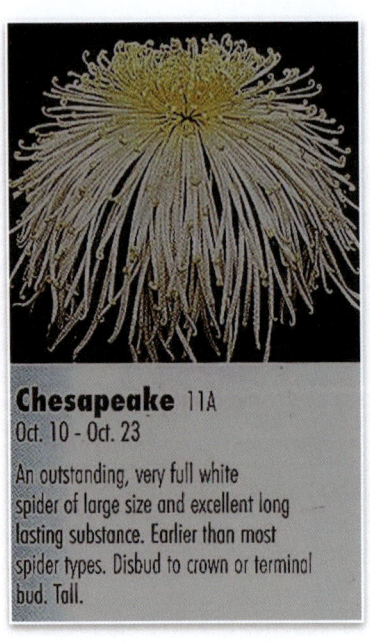

Every January a new edition of the *Kings Mums* catalog goes online. I love this catalog because the rooted mum cuttings are organized by class, and the information for each cultivar's name, bloom dates, and height are included. Rooted cuttings can be ordered from February through June every year. The picture on the left is taken from a Class 11, Spiders page in a *Kings Mums* catalog.

The name of this cultivar is "Chesapeake." It is an 11A Spider bloom. The "11" is the bloom class, and the "A" refers to the bloom size. Size "B" or "C" cultivars will produce smaller flowers. "October 10 - October 23" are the dates between which the cultivar will be in mature bloom. Description: "An outstanding, full white spider of large size and excellent long lasting substance. Earlier than most spider types." *Kings Mums* catalog says the bloom should be grown as a disbud (one flower). Don't worry about what "crown or terminal bud" means yet.

---

[2] http://www.mums.org/More/FAQs

"Tall" means the plant will grow to be from 5 - 7 feet tall. Rooted cuttings need to be planted after the danger of frost has passed.

Wait until late spring to order your rooted cuttings. If you plant them before July, the mums will bloom in time for show exhibitions at the dates noted in the catalog. You can place your order online or by mail and pay with either a check or credit card. Orders need to be received at Kings Mums a minimum of three weeks prior to shipping.

Kings Mums ships orders each Monday from March through June. An order takes 2 - 3 days to arrive. The rooted cuttings are sent via USPS Priority Mail. The cuttings arrive in plastic bags protected by Styrofoam peanuts, with each cultivar identified with a plastic strip. It is most important that your plants be removed from the plastic shipping bags immediately upon arrival.

The cuttings you receive will be 3 - 4 inches tall, and need to be planted as soon as possible into 4-inch pots in potting soil mix for the first two weeks. Be sure to keep the plastic label strip around the plant's stem. I always add a plastic label that is easier to read to the pot. I use white labels for disbuds and blue labels for sprays. That keeps me from disbudding my sprays later in the season.

Initial watering should be with a 30-10-10 liquid fertilizer, diluted to half strength. You can also add SuperThrive (a concentrated solution of vitamins and hormones used to encourage plant growth) using ¼ teaspoon to a gallon of water to the initial water/fertilizer mixture.

Set newly-planted rooted mum cuttings into trays and let them absorb the water. If watering with a hose, ensure that the cuttings are sitting up straight in the pot. You can use 12-inch bamboo skewers to support the plant. Place cuttings outside in moderate temperatures in a place protected from strong wind. Keep out of hot sun for a few days.

| 10-inch pot | 6-inch pot | 4-inch pot | 2-inch pot |

In three-to-four weeks, when your purchased, rooted plants have a well-developed root system and are 6 - 10 inches tall, transfer them into 6-inch pots. After about a month, transfer the plants into 10-inch pots, where they will mature and bloom. You can add ¼ teaspoon of SuperThrive to a gallon of water every time you transfer them into larger pots. In fact, it's okay to use SuperThrive when you weekly use water-soluble fertilizer on your plants. Add a small amount of soil to the bottom of the new pot. Place about ¼ teaspoon of Osmocote (a beaded fertilizer) on top of the soil, then set the rooted cutting on top of it. Fill in soil around the cutting. Be sure to wash off both the top and bottom sides of leaves regularly.

For insect control, it is important to apply a systemic that contains *imidacloprid* to the root system in the early spring before insect damage occurs. Sprays that contain *spinosad* help control bagworms, borers, beetles, caterpillars, moths, loopers, leaf miners, spider mites, tent caterpillars, and thrips can used up to six times during the growing season.

Chrysanthemum plants may also be grown in the ground. Place rooted plants fifteen inches apart in the sun and they will also develop good flowers.[3]

---

[3] **View video: Pat Stockett Johnston YouTube: Growing Chrysanthemums: Making Cuttings and Transferring to Larger Pots**

How to Plant Cuttings from Last Year's Mums

One rooted mum plant will cost $3.50 or more if ordered from *Kings Mums* catalog. A free way to get new cuttings is to take them from the new growth (stolen) that rooted from mum plants grown the previous year.

Steps for Taking Cuttings

Step 1: When the weather turns warm enough, usually in April in Southern California (but it could be later in other places) snip off 4-5 inches from the new growth in one of last year's mum pots. Remove the bottom 2-4 leaves. Keep 3-4 leaves on the top of the new cutting. If the only new growth is on old stems, you can use that to make cuttings also.

Step 2: Some growers dip the cutting top in a half-strength mixture of a liquid fungicide to kill off critters that may be hiding on its leaves. Some dip cutting tops in water containing SuperThrive, a vitamin-hormone mixture that stimulates root growth, using ¼ teaspoon to a gallon of water.

Pot with Stolon (new growth)

Step 3: Then dip the cutting's stem tip into either a liquid rooting solution like Dip'N Grow or a powdered rooting hormone about 1/3 of an inch deep. I shake off any extra rooting hormone, as too much slows down the root development. Now the cutting is ready to be planted in a 2" pot in purchased potting soil to which I have added perlite.

Step 4: You don't want the powdered rooting hormone to be scraped off when the cutting stem is pushed into the soil, so use a pencil to make a hole in the soil, insert the stem into the hole, and gently move soil around the stem. Weekly use a weak fertilizer on the new cutting as they root so they grow to their potential.

Another way to root stolon cuttings is to place four of them in a 4-inch pot. Notice only one label has been placed in this pot. When the successfully rooted cuttings are transferred to their own 4-inch pot, be sure to label each plant.

I use one color of label for disbud cuttings, and another color for spray cuttings. No matter how long you grow chrysanthemums, you will not be able to identify mum cultivars by their leaves. I generally toss plants that have lost their labels.

Step 5: Place newly planted mum cuttings into a tray of water in which SuperThrive has been added, using ¼ teaspoon to a gallon of water to the water mixture. Remove the cuttings from the water as soon as the soil is moist, but not saturated. Set away from direct sun for a few days.

The cuttings will root about two weeks quicker if you provide bottom heat for the soil by using heating mats or heating cables. These may be purchased online. Be sure and follow the directions included with the mat/cables.

When to Transfer Plants into Larger Pots

Whether a stolen cutting starts out in a 2-inch or 4-inch pot, each new rooted cutting not started with bottom heat will need to be transferred alone into a 4-inch pot in about four weeks, or after roots are showing down the side of the plant. I dump a slightly dry plant out of the pot and into my hand to check out root growth.

When the plant's roots have been established enough to transfer, put some soil in a 4-inch pot and form a shape using a 2-inch pot to make a hole for the transferred plant. Add ¼ teaspoon of Osmocote in the bottom of the hole. Transfer the plant and gently fill up the sides of the pot with soil. That way, the cutting's roots will not be damaged during the transfer process. In about a month, when the roots are ready, transfer the cultivar into a 6-inch, and then finally into a 10-inch pot, in which it will grow to maturity.

You may wonder why some growers don't plant their exhibition mums in the ground. It's because they want to turn the mum plants 90 degrees on a regular basis so that the blooms don't bend over from facing the sun and the leaves develop on all sides of the stems.

However, rooted mum cuttings can be grown in the ground in the sun. Be sure to plant at least fifteen inches apart, as many grow 5 - 7 feet high. You can stake and disbud these plants. Or you can plant them separately, at least 3 feet apart, and they will grow into bushes that fill your garden with multiple, small blooms and satisfy your grower's heart.

Before rooting your own stolon cuttings, check to be sure the cultivars are not copyrighted. *Kings Mums* catalog flags copyrighted mum cultivars.

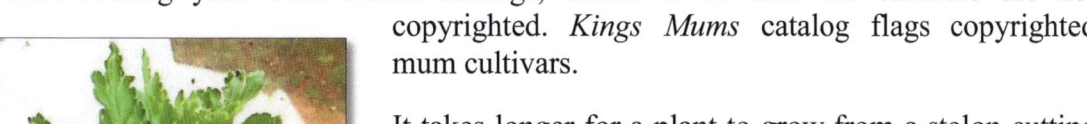

It takes longer for a plant to grow from a stolon cutting than it does from a rooted cutting. The rate of growth depends a lot depends on nighttime temperatures. It usually takes 4 - 5 weeks for my not heated stolon cuttings to produce a strong enough root system to transfer them to a 4-inch pot.

The plant in this picture looks big enough to transfer to a 4-inch pot. But it's hard to judge, just by looking at it, if the root growth is sufficient enough to need a transfer.

To check if the root system of a plant is developed enough to be transferred into a larger pot, dump a fairly dry plant out to check for root growth. You should see roots climbing down the side of the plant to the bottom of the plant before transferring it to a larger pot. This picture is of the roots of a plant from a 6-inch pot being transferred to a 10-inch pot.

New chrysanthemum growers often ask: "Why can't I start my plant cuttings in a 10-inch pot to begin with?"

Obviously, it would save a lot of time if you could eliminate transferring plants from 2-inch, to 4-inch, to 6-inch, and to the final 10-inch pot if your cuttings could start out in a 10-inch pot. But plant cuttings won't thrive if they are placed in 10-inch pots to begin with.

Using a 6-inch pot to shape a 10-inch pot hole

Plants need to grow roots down along the side of the pots in order to produce a strong root system. But the roots grow sideways first. So both a new-growth, stolon cutting or a purchased rooted cutting need to start out in a pot narrow enough for the roots to reach the sides of the pot early in their growth.

Some growers add a tablespoon of Epson Salts to the top soil around the plant when they transfer plants to 6" and 10" pots. Epson Salts contain hydrated magnesium sulfate, which are two elements crucial to plant growth. A tablespoon of Epson Salts can be spread on the soil around plants with yellow leaves, too, as it unlocks the nitrogen they need to start growing and greening. Adding Epson Salts to plant soil in the fall can also help with the foliage and color of the blooms. It is important to water the plants immediately after the Epson Salts is spread on the soil.

Chapter 3: June - July

Pinching the Stems

The months of June and July have important tasks that must be done if growing chrysanthemums for garden, cut flowers, or show exhibitions. First of all, as the mums develop sufficient roots, the plants need to be transferred into larger pots – either 4-inch, 6-inch, or 10-inch pots – depending on their size and root growth.

2-inch Pot   **4-inch Pot**   **6-inch Pot**   **10-inch Pot**

When chrysanthemum growers describe pots as being 2-inch, 4-inch, 6-inch, or 10-inch, they are not talking about the height of the pot. They are talking about the diameter of the pot. The measurements aren't exact, but are understood by all chrysanthemum growers.

Preventing Loss of Soil in 10-inch Pots

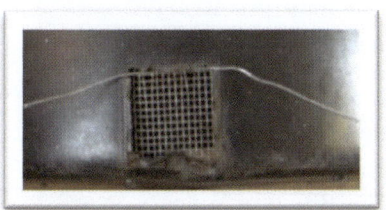

A big problem with the 10-inch pots is that some of them have very large drainage holes. Of course drainage holes are necessary. Otherwise the plant roots would sit in water and rot. But with this large of a drainage hole the water carries out soil, and eventually tunnels may occur. Then water flows straight to the drainage hole and the plant isn't evenly watered.

We tried placing a screen inside the pot with a strip of wire inserted on the outside of the pot to keep the soil from escaping. It helped a little. The best way to keep a tunnel developing in your soil is to not let the soil dry out enough to pull away from the side. I can tell if my pots need to be watered by how heavy or light a pot feels when I pick it up. If soil is dry half-way down the pot it needs watering.

I recently viewed a picture where someone had placed a coffee filter in the bottom of a pot to keep the soil from washing away during the watering process. Because it would be a quick solution to our losing soil with our 10-inch pots, I decided to order filters online of the size to fit a 10-gallon coffee urn. Compared to my 12-cup coffee filter pictured on the right, they are huge!

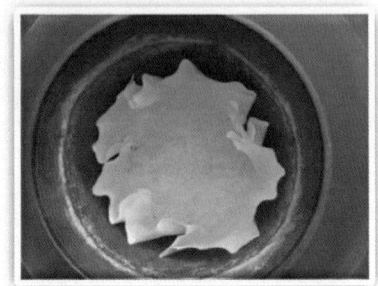

In fact, this huge filter measures 8 inches in height and 9 inches across the bottom. It fits perfectly into the bottom of my 1-gallon pots. But the filter certainly does not need to be 8 inches high. So I folded the filter in half, then took scissors and trimmed the filter height to about 4 inches. I will not worry about soil being lost through the drainage holes this year. In transplanting to 10-inch pots, drop the pot to make the soil force the air pockets out after the soil and plant are in place.

Pinching Back Mum Plant Stems

No matter which state you live in, each mum plant needs to have its stem pinched back (pruned), leaving less than 6 leaves on the stems, at least one time during the growing season. For either purchased rooted mums or new-growth stolon cuttings potted in March or April, the first pinch occurs around June 1. Depending on where you live, the early starters may need a second stem pinch between June 20 – July 1. For plants rooted in May or June, the first pinch is taken July 1. Plants will have only one tall stem to pinch the first time. After the first pinch, a mum plant should be allowed grow no more than three stems per plant for disbuds. Cultivars grown as sprays can have more than 3 stems.

Pinching Back a Mum Plant with One Stem

Let's begin with a plant with one tall stem. Pinching it back will control when the plant blooms and allow it to produce more stems. You want a mum plant in a 10-inch pot to have only 3 stems for disbuds. Four-five stems are possible for plants grown as sprays.

Each leaf on a stem will produce a new stem. Pinch a tall plant like this so that three strong leaves remain. The leaves should be facing in different directions away from the main stem.

This picture shows how the plant stem will look after being pinched back. Notice that, where the large leaf meets the stem, a small leaf is growing. The place where a new leaf grows out of the stem is called the *leaf node* in botanical terms. This small, new leaf will produce a stem that I will stake and grow one flower on. Notice that a little stem was left sticking up beyond the top leaf. This short part of the stem will support the new, top stem.

Pinching Back a Three-Stem Mum Plant

This plant received its first stem pinch in late May. As the plant matured, it was necessary to choose the three strongest stems on the plant and remove the extra stems. Picture #3 shows a plant with 3 stems that need pinching. Around July 1 the 3 stems on this plant were pinched back.

Carefully decide the best place to pinch a stem. Find a healthy leaf that is pointing toward the direction you want the new stem to grow. Picture #4 shows this plant after pinching the stems. Notice that the top leaf on each stem is growing away from the center of the pot.

Picture #5 is of a single stem on the pot with three large leaves. Notice how the top leaf this stem is growing towards the outside of the pot.

It is important to continue to weekly fertilize your mum plants. Water the plants as needed. One way to tell if a plant needs watering is to pick up the pot. If it is light in weight, it needs watering. On hot days it is good to mist the leaves. Continue to spray for insects and worms.

The August chapters describe how to stake every mum plant's stem so it will grow straight and help to support the weight of the single bloom that it will produce.[4]

---

[4] View video: Pat Stockett Johnston YouTube - Growing Chrysanthemums in July: Pinching Mums

Chapter 4: August

Why and How to Stake and Disbud Mum Plants

The month of August has important tasks that must be completed when growing chrysanthemums for home or exhibition shows. Each potted mum plant explodes with new growth in August, causing the stems to grow taller. Instead of shooting straight up, taller stems start to bend or curl, or get tangled up with stems from their own pot or those pots nearby. To ensure straight stems, every mum stem needs to be staked.

How to Stake a Chrysanthemum Stem

Chrysanthemum growers generally leave three stems on their mum plants, and allow only one bloom to mature per stem. By July 1, all mum plant stems have been pinched back, leaving only 3 strong, healthy leaves per stem. By the end of August, after the stems are tall enough (12 - 15 inches), each stem needs to be pulled to the side of the pot and tied to a 4 - 5 foot stake.

Great care must be taken during this process, for a still young stem can easily snap off as it's being tied to a stake, or the fragile leaves can easily be broken off or damaged. Mum blooms submitted in show exhibitions are judged on not just the flower, but also the leaves and stems.

In this picture of a staked stem, 5-inch plastic ties were used to fasten the stem to the stake. (You can use shorter ties.) If you are right-handed, place the stem on the left side of the stake, carefully fold the tie above a leaf that has already been disbudded, and twist the tie two times. The ties will stick straight out after you twist them. Don't leave them that way. Push the tie ends flat against the stake so that they don't intrude on the growth pattern of adjacent leaves.

This is a mum plant with three staked stems. Notice the stakes are placed in a triangular pattern, with each stake separated by an equal distance. It's also important to insert the stake as straight as you can into the pot. Your mum plant stems weren't born to lean. The stems' DNA insists that they grow straight up. Don't make your mum plants fight their natural tendencies with slanting stakes.

Difference in Terminal Bud and Crown Bud

Instructions for growing chrysanthemums for home and show often refer to terminal and crown buds. Here's the definitions for those from the *National Chrysanthemum Society Show and Judges Handbook.*[5]

Terminal Bud: "A chrysanthemum bud which has grown from inception to maturity without substantial interruption in development." This type of bud grows on a plant stem that has not been pinched, usually as a single stem plant in a wide 6-inch pot.

The Fukusuke bloom in this picture is an example of a flower grown on a terminal bud. Its single stem was not pinched. Instead, B9 was applied to the plant during the growing season to keep the stem under 16 inches in height. The plant foliage should be to the soil line. A Fukusuke is entered as a container-grown plant in an exhibition show.

---

[5]*Beginner's Handbook: Handbook for New Growers of Chrysanthemums, Revised Edition,* 2001. National Chrysanthemum Society, INC. USA. Website: www.mums.org

Crown Bud: "A chrysanthemum bloom bud resulting from an interruption in the vegetative growth of the plant." This means the bloom grew on a stem that had been pinched. Most blooms will be grown on a crown bud. The picture to the right is a container-grown set of three of the spider "Seatons Galaxy" grown on crown buds.

How to Disbud Auxiliary Buds on a Chrysanthemum Stem

August growth doesn't only include the stems. New leaves also grow on the stems as they get taller. Mum plants want to produce blooms, so every new leaf will support the growth of a lateral that will produce an auxiliary bud. If left unchecked, the auxiliary bud will produce a limp stem with many small blooms.

Because this mum plant is being grown to produce large blooms for show exhibitions, each of its three stems can only be allowed to produce one bloom. That means that, except for the terminal bud growing at the top of the stem, all the auxiliary buds and lateral growth must be removed. This removal process is called "disbudding." It's really another type of pruning.

This picture demonstrates two new lateral stems growing on a plant. The lateral stem on the left is fairly young. The lateral growth to the right has larger leaves sticking straight up. Lateral growth needs to be removed as soon as possible, either by snapping off with your fingers or clippers.

Sometimes the lateral growth on a leaf will quickly produce a new flower bud that needs to be immediately removed. Why? That bud is sucking strength from your plant that needs to go to the top, terminal bloom. I remove the auxiliary buds by using a small pair of embroidery scissors. I place my thumb under the leaf on which the bud is growing, support the stem with my forefinger, lift up the bud with the scissors, then carefully push the scissors upwards. I try to avoid digging a deep hole in the stem or scratching the stem during this process.[6]

---

[6] View video: Pat Stockett Johnston YouTube - Growing Chrysanthemums: August Tasks

Notice the new stems in this picture are growing very low on the plant stem. Break them off where they join the stem or remove them with clippers.

Of course watering, fertilizing, and spraying for insect control are also included in August tasks. Yes, growing mums for home enjoyment or show an exhibition does take a lot of time. But no, it isn't work. I always enjoy the peace that falls over me as I perform the necessary tasks that will eventually produce beautiful chrysanthemum blooms for October and November exhibition shows.

August Catastrophe in My Chrysanthemum Garden

A catastrophe happened in my chrysanthemum garden one year. The kind of catastrophe all home or show chrysanthemum growers dread—the loss of a beautiful mum bloom.

I can hear you thinking now. "The loss of one of those little button chrysanthemums? Dozens of blossoms still remain. Why would losing a bloom you're growing to show matter?"

It's easy to reply to that question. The garden variety of chrysanthemum grows naturally with no pinching. But the 13 classes of chrysanthemums cultivated specifically for exhibition shows are limited to three blooms per pot. It's sad to lose one.

My catastrophe happened unexpectedly, while carefully working my way through a row of 10-inch mum pots. I've perfected my technique. Moving each pot to a low table, I turn it 360 degrees and disbud unwanted, new lateral growth.

Why? Because stringent guidelines for growing chrysanthemums for exhibition shows state that only a single bloom may be grown on each stem. Of course, that one bloom should be growing at the top of the stem. The bloom stem needs to be cut 22-inches high to show.

After disbudding all the unwanted new laterals, I carefully tied new stem growth to a stake. That's so the stem will be straight (another show winner) and the heavy body of the single blossom can have support as it matures.

While carrying the pot back to its place I accidentally brushed against another bloom. The snapping sound of a stem breaking stopped me in my tracks. My worst fears were realized. I'd knocked off the top of a beautifully growing stem, its top ready to soon explode with a show-worthy chrysanthemum.

For a moment I stood there and grieved for what might have been a winning blossom.

Looking for Comfort

I decided to memorialize the event by taking a picture of the poor, beheaded stem. Then I went into the house, broken mum tip in hand, to commiserate with my husband. Unfortunately, he's not the commiserating type.

"That's too bad," he said, almost flippantly. No sign of remorse or sorrow in his voice. His shoulders didn't sag. No tears came to his eyes.

Then his face brightened. "I can tell you how to get over it."

In disbelief I raised an eyebrow. "Really?"

He grinned. "Go back outside and play with the 500 others blooms you're cultivating."

I gave my heart-hardened husband a dirty look, walked outside, and tossed my catastrophe into the garbage can, determined to never experience that type of problem again. At least, not that day.

Chapter 5: September

Taking Care of Mum Plants Leaves, Stems, and Buds

If you are growing chrysanthemums for home or shows in the States, the September tasks will involve the leaves, the stems, and the buds.

Leaf Control

Notice how the leaf is hugging the stake. This is a common problem in growing chrysanthemums for home or show. It's necessary to go on "leaf patrol" every day, looking for leaves that are hugging their stakes for two reasons.

First of all, when a leaf hugs a stake it changes its shape and causes the leaf to not hang right when the plant is removed from the stake. So it's important to make daily walks up and down the rows of plants looking for leaf stake huggers. Often just carefully moving the leaf to the right or left side of the stake fixes the problem.

Secondly, a leaf hugging a stake can negatively influence the angle in which the stem grows. Straight stems are one of the elements judges use when awarding blue, red, or yellow ribbons in show competitions. The way to fix it is to move the leaf to the side on which it lays naturally. Then the stem needs to be carefully tied to the stake every 6-12 inches.

You can leave what I call a "track" between the stem and the stake to give the stem room to grow without catching on the stake or leaving indentations on the stem. That also facilitates disbudding new buds at leaf *axils* (the angle between the upper side of a leaf or stem and the supporting stem or branch).

21

Worms and Other Creepy Crawlies

From September on is the prime time for worms and pests to devour the fruits of your labor, for they love fresh-blooming buds. This green, mums-destroying worm didn't realize his demise was near. It's best to check for unwanted creatures in the cool of the morning or evening before they hide out under a leaf. Continue to control insects, pests, worms, and fungus infections by regular spraying.

One Bud Remaining at Tip of Each Stem

As in this picture of a green bud, in September have all the blooms you plan to show as disbuds or cut flowers down to just the one crown bud at the tip of the stem. That means carefully disbudding the unwanted new growth on all of your plants on a regular basis. It's also important to turn potted mum plants 90 degrees every 3 - 4 days so that the leaf growth is the same on all sides of the stem. If a stem is more than 4 inches higher than the last tie, I like to add a tie to the stake. Some growers add new ties ever 6-12 inches. It's up to you.

September is a month of waiting and watching for those green pea-like crown buds to mature and show color. After a month of leaf patrol, spraying, staking, and disbudding, October and November blooms will make all your labors worthwhile.

Epsom Salts consist of Magnesium sulfate, two elements crucial to plant growth. They can be sprinkled around a plant's stem base on the soil if you feel your soil is deficient in this mineral. Water immediately after adding Epsom Salts to the top soil. [7]

---

[7] View video: Pat Stockett Johnston YouTube - Growing Chrysanthemums: September/October Tasks

More Failures

Despite the hours spent with my 188 pots of chrysanthemums grown for cut flowers and exhibition shows one year, more mum failures occurred.

1. Bloom Matured Too Early

The picture of the Class 4 Decorative mum *Olympia* in the *Kings* catalog was beautiful. Quickly I checked out the time span in which the flower was supposed to bloom: Oct. 15 - October 28.

The Orange County Chrysanthemum Society Show was to be held the last weekend in October, so those dates seem like good bloom times for entries for that show.

An *Olympia* mum cutting from *King's Mums* catalog arrived June first. I became a little anxious when Olympia's crown buds began to grow in late July. The flower matured at a rapid speed. White color showed in the bud the middle of August. In the middle of September, when Olympia's 6-inch wide, white petals sparkled against the dark green of its leaves, the bloom was ready to show. But alas, six weeks too early for an exhibition show. Its early bloom made that cultivar a failure. Friends were gifted with its blooms instead, much to their delight.

2. Insect Infestation: My husband Gordon is in charge of watering, fertilizing, and spraying our mums for insects and worms. Every week he faithfully dons his white mask and long sleeves, armed with multiple varieties of fertilizer and insect spray. He not only sprays our mums for unwanted pests, but all the flowers in our garden and the neighbors' shrubs that grow along our common fence.

I walk through the garden every day looking for signs of aphids or worm intruders on my mum plants stems and buds. One day I discovered a plant stem covered with black, moving insects. Some crawled along the stem. Others munched on fresh buds and leaves.

Grabbing a spray bottle of insecticide, I drenched the creatures, and then washed off the bug remains with water. One insect, dead or alive on a submitted mums show bloom, limits its ability to win a ribbon. Preventing bug infestations was a failure. Our plants needed to be sprayed for insects more often—perhaps even every five days, instead of weekly.

3. More Worms

A few nasty, green, bud-devouring worms took up residence in some early chrysanthemum bloomers in September. They did it quietly—not a squeak from those fat worms revealed their hidden existence deep into a *Candid* Class 3, Intermediate Incurve bud. It was only as I moved its pot to check for new, unwanted growth around the roots that the two criminals showed their ugly heads. Then they had the nerve to reveal their whole bulging bodies—bodies bursting from a feast of young *petals* (botanical term: florets).

A close look at the attacked bud made my heart pound. Only stubs of florets remained around the edges of one side of the chrysanthemum bud. Those terrible creatures were headed straight for the bud's center. A wail of misery and woe filled the air. It came straight out of my mouth.

What to do? My blood ran hot and furious. Kill the enemy! Do it now! Common sense caused me to pause a moment. With my bare hands? Never! No one wants squished worm guts on their hands. I went into the house and got a paper napkin, then came out and captured both invaders. Two dead worms with one pinch. Vindicated.

The sad truth? This worms-eaten *Candid* bud would never mature into a judge-worthy bloom. It had to be untied from its stake. Its 30-inch stem cut down to about six inches in height. My sweet husband came outside to find out what the entire ruckus was about. He assured me that, in order to kill any worm survivors, he would spray all my thriving chrysanthemum plants with BT (*Bacillus thuringiensis)* right away.

Winners or not, each mum bloom is beautiful, a gift reflecting God's creative genius. Their splendor is what makes time spent caring for them so enjoyable.

4. Hot Water

One summer we had a plumber install a large sink in our back yard. It enabled my husband to mix fertilizer, insecticides, and BT in the garden, instead of the kitchen sink. The plumber mentioned that he'd piped the sink near the hot water heater. We didn't pay much attention to his comment.

When it hit 109 degrees in our back yard that year, I went out to water our chrysanthemum plants. We have a hose attachment that offers a variety of water choices: cone, center, flat, jet, soaker, mist, or shower.

Because it was such a hot day, leaves and buds were gently showered. After about 30 seconds I ran my hand through the water. It was hot! My hand jerked away from the water and I moved the showering water stream to the ground. But it was too late. The leaves, stems, and new buds of several chrysanthemum plants experienced death by water so hot it cooked the life right out of their leaves and buds.

Walking through the rows of mums the next day, I beheld the terrible damage that hot shower had inflicted on innocent, growing-nicely-as-you-please chrysanthemum plants. Lesson learned? Run the water from the sink hose long enough to empty it of its hot sun or water heater water.

In fact, it is wise to always check the temperature of the water coming from your hose when you first turn it on.

5. Very Tall Plants

To solve a chrysanthemum-growing height problem we bought a bar stool.

Some of my spoon, spider, and spray chrysanthemum plants had grown to over five feet tall. Sitting on my folding chair to disbud or adjust the stake to support the bloom would not allow me see the top of the plant. With 188 pots of mums, that meant too much standing up for Grandma Pat.

My husband suggested throwing away the tall plants. But I consider destroying a living chrysanthemum plant an act of murder.

Perhaps a bar stool seat would be high enough for me to remain seated when working on tall mum plants.

During a visit to Big Lots my husband spotted barstools in the furniture department. We rushed over to check them out. One stool had a metal frame and fabric-covered seat. We liked its $35.00 price. The stool even had a back on it that swiveled. "I can cover the seat with plastic quite easily," said my husband. Which he did.

Shaded and Staked August Mum Plants

Problem solved! My choice of seat heights when I work on my chrysanthemums? The low folding chair or the 30-inch high barstool. Who would have thought a barstool could make a gal this happy?

Chapter 6: October
Staking and Disbudding Plants with Blooms

Time for Chrysanthemum Colors to Appear

When growing chrysanthemums for show, October is a time of anticipation and delight as the green buds burst forth in an array of colors.

Time to Remove All But One Bud

An important October task is the disbudding of unwanted flower buds. The picture to the left is a good example of how buds form at the top of a stem. The center bud should be the one to mature. The other buds must be removed (disbudded) as soon as possible for two reasons. They pull energy from the center bud that inhibits its size and, if I wait any longer, when I remove the bud it will leave a scar whose size depends on the thickness of the stem. Large disbud scars lose points in an entry to an exhibition show.

Go on a "new bud patrol" every day in October. Removing a bud, though literally killing new growth, will result in larger blooms.

Time to Check Every Stem, Top-to-Bottom

New buds don't just grow at the top of the stem. Every leaf produces a new bud at its node. Often the buds at the bottom of the stem pop out after the buds on top show up. You can see a bud that needs to be disbudded on the left of the plant stem. Lift every potted chrysanthemum plant onto a small table once a week and turn it 360 degrees to check for new, unwanted buds. Begin checking at the bottom of the plant and look at every leaf all the

way to the top on every stem, disbudding new growth as you go with a pair of embroidery scissor for small buds. Or, if the bud has a stem longer than an inch, gently push the stem to the side between finger and thumb and it will pop off.

Time to Stake Chrysanthemum Stems

Because chrysanthemum plants have tall stems and large blooms, each stem on every plant must be staked. The young bloom in this picture illustrates how I added an elevator stake to the original stake that can be moved up and support the bud as it grows. A stake also helps a stem grow straight, a very important aspect when show mums are judged. It supports the heavy weight of the blooms and helps the bloom grow flat (not bending in one direction).

When the bloom is placed in a show vase, the supporting stake is removed, as show mums cannot be staked in their vases. If you intend to enter mums in an exhibition show, the importance of staking each chrysanthemum plant stem as it matures cannot be overemphasized.

Waiting for Chrysanthemums Blooms to Mature

Here's a picture of Spider and Reflex mums in my garden the middle of October. These plants will have huge flowers whose blooms may measure anywhere from 4 to 8 inches in height and 4 to 14 inches in diameter. Notice in the picture that I have staked each stem, and the blooms are supported by a secondary, elevator stake. Most of these blooms need 2 - 3 more weeks to mature.

If growing mums is for your own enjoyment, cut a bloom at any stage of maturity. However, show blooms need to be at least 85% mature. Chrysanthemum Exhibition Shows are scheduled across the States beginning in October, with the Phoenix Chrysanthemum Society Show the third week of November. Check the show schedule on the National Chrysanthemum Society Website at www.mums.org to find dates for local National Chrysanthemum Society Shows. The annual National Chrysanthemum Society Show rotates every other year between a west coast and an east coast state.

Chapter 7: October - November

How to Cut and Prepare Chrysanthemums for Exhibition Shows

In my first year of growing chrysanthemums, I had no idea when to cut or how to prepare chrysanthemums for exhibition shows. Organizing what must be done into a few basic steps now makes the task less daunting.

Choosing the Right Bloom

1. The week before a chrysanthemum show, stroll through the potted chrysanthemums and look for blooms that are mature, have bright colors, and are large-sized. I grow three stems in each 10-inch pot. It's rare for the three blooms on a plant to mature at the same time. Sometimes one plant will give me a bloom for three different shows. Blooms may be cut 2 - 4 days before a show date.

Cutting the Stem the Correct Height

2. Two to three days before a show I cut a bamboo stake 23 inches long and mark it with blue masking tape to make it easy to identify. I use that stake to measure the stem length before I cut it. Be careful not to knock off any leaves when clipping the stem.

Hydrating the Cut Bloom

3. It is important to hydrate the chrysanthemum blooms before putting them in their travel containers. Do not remove the leaves from the bloom's stem. Carefully place the cut bloom in a large container without submerging the bloom itself. I use a garbage can. Allow a chrysanthemum bloom to hydrate at least an hour before placing it in its travel bottle or bucket. This hydration process prevents the bloom from wilting during travel and helps keep it fresh-looking when being judged.

4. Place the bloom in a glass bottle filled with water that has been treated with bleach. The bottle opening should be wide enough to hold the stem and the stake.

5. Tie the bloom's show entry card with a tie to the top of the bottle or to the bucket handle. (Every bloom is submitted with an entry card.)

6. Place 3 to 4 bottles holding mum blooms in a 5-gallon bucket. Separate the bottles with wadded newspaper.

7. I store the buckets with flowers in them in a sheltered place until travel day. Here they are in my living room.

Safe Mums Traveling Strategies

How to Protect the Stems and Blooms During Transport

Once the mums are cut and hydrated, it's time to prepare them for transport. Some growers use this technique. Duct-tape 18-inch bamboo stakes on the outside of a 5-gallon bucket. Fill the bucket with three inches of water. Place a bloom in the bucket beside a taped-on stake and fasten each bloom stem to the stake using plastic ties. Protect large blooms by supporting them with paper plates. Many growers have great success with this transport system, but I often removed or damaged leaves in the tying-untying process.

Another Unsuccessful Transporting-to-Show Process

Cut the stakes tied to stems, hydrate the blooms with the stakes still tied to the stems, and place the blooms still tied to the stake into the bottles, 3 - 4 blooms per bucket.

At first we transported the buckets in the back of our van to show venues. But the buckets shifted in the van, causing the blooms to brush against each other and knock off florets (petals). I'm sure you understand that judges prefer a full bloom—not one with patches of petals missing. But we found that even staked to the top of the stem, the weight of the blooms caused them to brush against other blooms in their own buckets, resulting in damaged petals.

Better Chrysanthemum Transporting-to-Show Process

Now I have developed my own tried-and-true method of transporting chrysanthemums to shows, still using 5-gallon buckets. But I've added 18-inch bamboo stakes, glass water bottles, wadded newspaper, and bleach to my supplies. Here's the process.

1. Remove a hydrated chrysanthemum bloom from its soaking bath. (Start the hydrating process 2 - 3 days before the show).
2. Remove leaves from the bottom twelve inches of the stem.
3. Carefully tie an 18-inch stake high enough to support the chrysanthemum bloom onto the stem.

The Perfect Transport Solution

Though greatly pleased with my new method of preparing the blooms for travel to a show, we still lost blooms in the transport process. I begged my creative husband to create some type of frame that would keep the buckets from moving around.

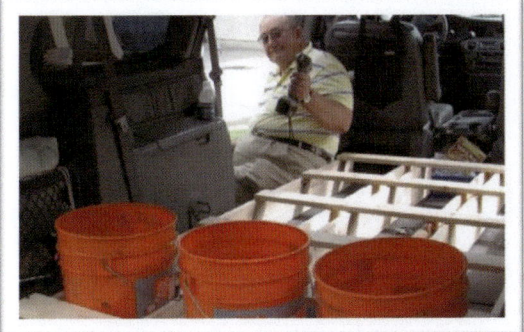

One day Gordon headed out to Home Depot, determined to buy the needed materials to build a frame that would hold the buckets.

He designed a wooden frame for our van that holds 15 buckets and keeps the buckets from bumping against one another in the transport process. After a show, we remove the form from the van, cover it in plastic, and store it in the back yard.

Not a single bloom has been lost since we started using this bloom transport method.

Chapter 8: October - November

How Chrysanthemum Blooms Are Judged

Judging the Descanso Chrysanthemum Society Show

After caring for chrysanthemum plants for six months, it's important to understand how to choose the best blooms to enter in show exhibitions. Judges use a 100-point scoring scale based on a perfect chrysanthemum bloom; the scale is published in the *National Chrysanthemum Society Show and Judges Handbook*. By far the greatest amount of chrysanthemum show entries will be a single chrysanthemum cultivars grown on one stem—a disbud.

Important Rules

Some important rules to follow when entering chrysanthemums for show exhibitions include:

1. All chrysanthemums must have been grown outdoors by the exhibitor.
2. Entered chrysanthemums may not have been shown in any previous show during the current year.
3. Only one entry for each cultivar variety may be submitted.
4. Disbudded chrysanthemum blooms must measure at least four inches in diameter except for pompon, brush, and thistle types, whose blooms are small.
5. A disbudded chrysanthemum bloom must measure between 18" to 30" in height from the table to the top of the bloom.

Point Scoring Scale for Chrysanthemum Disbuds

At a chrysanthemum show, judges measure four specific qualities of a disbudded bloom and take off points for imperfections.

1. Bloom quality (55 points total) – includes the color, form and fullness, size, substance, and freshness
2. Stem (10 points total) – includes size and substance, straightness, and the uniformity of the internodes
3. Foliage (leaves; 10 points total) – includes color, size, substance, and freshness
4. Exhibit as a Whole (25 points total) – includes, cleanliness, absence of damage, pose, and proportion

Ribbon Award Points

A blue ribbon award requires 90 or more points; red – 85 or more points; yellow – 80 or more points. A purple ribbon is given for the best bloom in a class (example: spider, spoon, quill, and pompon)

Pictures of Four "Best of Group" Chrysanthemums

It's beneficial to pay close attention to the judging point scale when choosing the blooms to enter into exhibition shows. The four disbuds in the photos below were judged the best cultivar in their group at the 2010 National Chrysanthemum Society show held in Corona Del Mar, California.

Saga Nishiki   **Evans Dream**   **Golden Splendor**   **Seatons Toffee**
Brush   **Spider**   **Spider**   **Quill**

Chapter 9: January - February
Winter Chrysanthemum Plant Care

The shows are over now. I've enjoyed giving away and making flower arrangements with the chrysanthemums that did not mature enough to show in October and November. In December my pot of mums are watered, sprayed, and fertilized as I want to keep them alive.

It might surprise you to learn that January and February chrysanthemum plant care will provide the plants that will grow this summer for home or chrysanthemum show exhibitions. In the truest of senses, the old plant dies back, bringing in the new growth used for cuttings for new plants. So what does January chrysanthemum plant care include? The following pictures describe January chrysanthemum plant care.

This Peach Wingfield, Class 2 Reflex bloom has been staked and disbudded. This bloom won a blue ribbon at an Exhibition Show.

Here's what my Peach Wingfield plant looked like the first week of January. The top bloom has completely died back. However, new blooms sprouted along the stem after I quit disbudding new growth in November.

The new blooms have a lighter peach color. Even the size of some of the blooms is show-worthy (4" diameter). But I still could never show these blooms. Why? The stems aren't thick enough to support the weight of the bloom, nor are the stems long enough to be displayed in a show vase (stems generally cut to 22 inches for show blooms).

In fact, the stems were too short to put the flowers in a short vase. The blooms were too pretty to throw away, so I removed the flowers, cut the stems off at the base of the flowers, and floated the chrysanthemums in a shallow bowl. It looked lovely on my kitchen table.

The first week of January prune the stems of all plants to 6 inches in height, leaving 6 - 8 leaves on each stem.

The old stems will die back and new growth (called stolon) rises from last year's mother plant. Most of the plants will produce stolon. If they don't, you can take cuttings from new growth on old stems.

I place my pruned plants on shelves in the backyard to make it easy to water, fertilize, and spray for bugs during January - April. If the pots are set on the ground you may experience a slug or snail invasion.

If the new growth starts to get too tall or the stems turn woody, prune back the new growth and wait six weeks after the prune before taking cuttings.

Although I'm a city girl, I must have a few farmer genes, as I love this whole January Chrysanthemum plant care process—this bringing continued life to what would, on its own, die out and disappear.

I take cuttings from new mum growth (stolen) when Southern California night temperatures are in the 60's—usually in late March or April. Check with a local chrysanthemum society to find out the best time to take cuttings in your area.

Using heating mats or heating cables will enable new cuttings to produce roots in about two weeks. Follow the instructions that accompany these types of plant propagation equipment. Cuttings from stolon may also be rooted in hothouses.

Ideally, take cuttings of medium diameter stolen growth. If your plants have no stolen growth, take cuttings from new shoots on the old stems. You won't notice much difference.

Enjoy these moments away from the time-consuming responsibilities during January and February. Prepare to start with new rooted cuttings ordered from *Kings Mums* or producing your own rooted cuttings from the new growth (stolon) from last year's plants.

Mums the Word!

Printed in Great Britain
by Amazon